Joan Darc

Joan Darc

NATHALIE QUINTANE

translated from

the French

by

SYLVAIN GALLAIS

and CYNTHIA HOGUE

LA PRESSE ❦ PROVIDENCE & PARIS

2017

Jeanne Darc by Nathalie Quintane
Copyright © 1998 P.O.L éditeur
Translation © 2017 Sylvain Gallais and Cynthia Hogue

Published in the United States by La Presse,
an imprint of Fence Books

La Presse/Fence Books are distributed by Consortium
www.cbsd.com
www.lapressepoetry.com

Quintane, Nathalie, 1964–
Translated from the French by Sylvain Gallais and Cynthia Hogue
Joan Darc/Nathalie Quintane
p.   cm.

ISBN 978-1-934200-71-1
1. French poetry. 2. Poetry. 3. Contemporary translation.

FIRST EDITION
10 9 8 7 6 5 4 3 2 1

We would like to give warm thanks to P.O.L for their generosity
in allowing us to publish this translation. The complete
list of P.O.L's marvelous books can be
viewed at www.pol-editeur.fr

Contents

Joanie!

Joan!

I am the saint on the airwaves

Catherine's voice in your ear

Others will speak through you

Joan, you are exceptional,
but you must fight to stay modest.

When men follow you
never forget to tell them of the Catholic faith

your knees will guide horses

Catherine creates Joan Darc

you'll never make it here

Joan, you must go to Vaucouleurs, meet
    Robert de Baudricourt, make him take you
        to Charles VII, persuade him of your mission,
        be placed at the head of a small army, force
    the English to lift the siege of Orleans, and
crown the king at Reims.

Your ears will guide your life

– From the center, you had a panoramic view of the whole flock; you never lost a sheep. All you had to do was turn around from time to time (but no shepherd works that way: a moving flock pulls him along in its path). Or you gazed at one of the four cardinal points, so the sun couldn't blind you but dazzled the sheep instead.

– From hilltops, you kept losing the furthest grazers.

– She'd practiced whistling to her dog.

– Her fear: that having taken her eyes off the flock, it'd be gone when she looked back.

– If she stared long enough into a sheep's eyes, it turned its head.

– So used to the backs of her sheep, she hated not seeing the horse's back unless mounted.

– She wondered if she'd feel her voice in ankle or anus when she spoke.

– By fifteen, she'd found a way to live by the statement:

–"Something must happen!"

– Burying her hands in the thick wool of a sheep's back made her less cold.

– Sometimes when her feet caught in her too-long and muddy skirt, the dog circled her, coughing.

– Joan loves herself when she's working. Even if some parts of her job of watching sheep are definitely work (rising at dawn, following the wandering flock, keeping an eye on the dog), most of the time, sitting on a rock or standing up to stretch, she doesn't feel like she's really working.

– When she sews, her mother calls it work, but not her father.

– When she follows the flock, her father calls that work, but not her mother (she calls it "strolling").

– Some of the villagers call her lazybones.

– For her, work has no particular location, like the baker has his oven or the blacksmith his forge.

– Since except for very young children everyone thinks he's working, and thinks others are working, too – even if not as hard – naturally she's considered part of this group, but she has only to change jobs (e.g. switch from spinning to weaving) for a thrill of relief to call everything into question: can someone be so happy and relaxed about the prospect of work? Is work a state of mind?

– Still, everyone around her seems to be really working.

– They mop their brows and complain.

– St. Catherine told her she had nothing to complain about.

– As a result, she does not seem to be working.

– And the others notice that she doesn't seem to be working.

Because Joan takes care of the sheep, their wool, her hair, the cooking, her nails, and the opinions of her neighbors, her future schedule is already set, there are things she must do as long as the neighbors gossip, as long as she has her hair, as long as her nails keep growing, and there are sheep with time to graze.

But there's *never* nothing to do, since there's *no* nothing, so there's always the chance to shear sheep, clip nails, respond to neighbors, devour a dish, more and more the things she does are making her more and more the person (Joan).

Like most of the villagers, who believe that the dauphin not yet dauphin must become so, Joan, who's still finding herself and believes the exact same thing, has trouble distinguishing herself clearly enough from the others so that she might claim the dauphin's accession to the throne as an incandescent cause or her inalienable duty.

Saying this dumbfounds her.

It seemed the voices would never give her a good enough kick in the ass to push her, to put her on a path she must follow to its end, an end we've already thoroughly discussed, to take on and to undertake the battles themselves, to rattle the powerful dedicated to a defeat redefined as a choice.

Only this idea that the dauphin, the true dauphin, was not *dauphin for all* proved, in the end, thanks to this rude error, unbearable enough to fire her up. Then she watched her anger rise toward that point where finally the unbearable makes everything ready to blow.

For her, there was:
– youth, a youth not given to moods, and endowed with character she could count on since childhood: supple body, instructive wounds, unstopped knowledge of illness and death, any azimuth soon dispersed;
– + models for anger from some of the angry, rare though numerous enough to dub the waiting of others a perfect torpor.

Here's how the future depends on your arguments.

While in Domrémy, and at an age when one word
is still as good as any other, you think a well-milked
cow, some babble, a pat on the head, are all you need
to show them who you are.

But once the tongue's untied, look out!
People love to trip up a gossip.

Viewed from the outside, a fatal separation, arranged from above by a fatal power in the form of sonorous and luminous cumulus.

Actually, in her first life she sewed miraculously well

but others considered this zeal for the supernatural to be an excessive care put into her work, maybe maniacal.

If she'd pursued her angelical studies in Domrémy as if they were nothing, nobody would have thought twice

but they took her leaving, and especially her not returning, as proof that she had *two lives.*

– Joan had no feeling of molting: exultant on horseback, she had no time to dwell on what she left behind, or on what she would find. Though her calling as prophet (but didn't she exaggerate that so she could leave?) carried her, a priori, wholly toward the future, the sudden break stuck her in the present, and it was in the present she counted on lifting the sieges, and making a dauphin out of the dauphin.

A groom makes a horse more of a horse. A lone horse, mastless in the tall grass of a field, refuses any link to the person watching him, but facing him, Joan feels a bit like she's growing a muzzle herself. There without introduction, she has no way to resist such power.

When the groom introduces the horse, a greeting is possible, which *places* her – children running and knocking about the village lanes, until they wave hello, simply aren't there.

Once the three have performed the social rituals, all horsey mischief fades: thanks to the groom, Joan's no longer tempted to be a horse, but also, thanks to the horse, she has no desire to be a groom, for she has become a third term, *the girl who rides horses.*

Dressed in armor, Joan spends a lot of her time study-
ing the different parts of this armor, piece by piece,
looking herself up and down, deciding whether to
first consider the plates of articulated metal that cover
her feet or those on her shoulders.

As she walks, she doesn't walk all of a piece, but
follows herself, independently, and by turns, in each
aspect of her new garb.

The same when wearing a new dress – she finds
herself reduced to her dress many days in a row, its
shape, weight, and color heavy on her mind.

Remade by the dress, Joan has no time to think of
anything else: to make plans or decisions. There is

not enough room to even obey orders.

Admiring herself in her new dress is paralyzing.
Regretting it, too.

(The same when she has just bathed, being clean
prevents her for a time from putting some distance
on cleanliness.)

– The sword's hilt is as important as its blade, not for its ornament, but because a sword without a hilt cannot be held, and because a murderous sword must be *firmly* held: its pommel should fill the space of the hand clenched around it.

He who holds fast to Durendal holds also the hand of Roland.

– The hilt of the sword that Joan would hold her whole life, was a prosthesis modeled after the original, close-fitted to serve (sword-hand).

– Whereas the sword's design, made to measure for the individual (size of the blade in proportion to the body, hilt drawn according to the shape of the hand), would first suggest a synthesis of Joan, frozen in brandishing gesture (sword-man).

Hers, she had chosen it *"dans un grand tas de ferraille,"* which is to say, out of a great deal of old iron.

Why when she's standing around with empty arms will people give her a wide berth, but when she's seated milking a cow or sewing a button do they stop just far enough away to watch what she's doing, as if that bit of her own past, getting caught at her chores, was so moving?

Why, how, does a simple action (rubbing down, polishing) not suffice?
Why, how, does a simple reflection (sound of rain, dust of dandelion) not suffice either?
What could make action more active, and reflection more reflective?

Surely having reached this stage of the question of reflection and action, anyone would think, right away, of going all out.

The militant of humility drinking the soup someone spat in.

The young monk plowing the furrow without rest.

Unprepared for this, or for waiting anymore, Joan will balance the mouths of the angels at her ear and her charger between her thighs, coupling action and reflection, until the rout.

– Before my first assault, there was a world between the world and me: bells tolled, my father yelled, sheep bleated.

She dreams up new forms of assault.

– Sadly, the number of military ruses is limited; at best, you get only a new combination of old ruses, one ruse fitted into another, or in an unexpected sequence.
– The way cities are built, they can only be attacked and captured in 7 ways: by the gate, an open gate, by the closed, staved-in gate, by scaling the walls, by knocking the walls down, by making a breach, from the top by throwing weapons, objects, ablaze, from below by digging a tunnel.
– By brandishing heads stuck on spears above the crenels, 8 ways.

Pyramid of Burgundian arms piled at the gates of Orleans
Confecting a sarcophagus to stop the stench

– I don't despair of adding to the repertory of ruses
one that will bear my name
Because the preparation for war gives me a taste for
invention.

It's a matter of making things concrete through action.

As my battles add up, my virginity expands.

– For the moment, I'm radical and spontaneous:
if you don't like the war, change wars.

– Since she made them sing Psalm 22 after every assault, the soldiers pillage less, though she doesn't forget that this song could just as easily lead to new levels of violence.

– These songs are also associated with a technique of breathing, which, raising and lowering the column of air from the abdomen to the neck, calms the mind at the same time as it develops thoracic capacity.

– When the nobles make confession with gloves on, she strikes their palms with the flat of her sword.

– In an army, especially a small one, no man's interchangeable with another. Each has his strength, according to which each belongs to one of three levels: *the energetic level*, which is on the ball, falls in step, the quickest and the first to strike up boombadaboom (Montjoie-Saint-Denis!) with the drums; *the practical level,* which sees to the comfort of the troops at rest, and connects them in the thick of battle; *the ambient level*, most of whom you can't make out, who are held in reserve following the vanguard, a more spontaneous level, but alert and ready – which no army could do without.

– In the head, throughout the assault, half an hour of Montjoie-Saint-Denis!, no break, and all blows to the beat of Montjoie-Saint-Denis!, one death, Montjoie, two, Saint-Denis!, a buckling horse: Montjoie, a skull: Saint-Denis!, a continuous sound like a buzzing in the head, drooling spit inside the helmet, teeth caved into gums.

Just as miming the gestures of eating won't feed you, so imitating a soldier's moves doesn't make you want to fight: you have to get used to the idea.

But no one gets used to a brazen idea if it doesn't create above all else a buzz that combats the other ideas.

This buzz spreads among troops before battle. Soldiers vibrate in unison, like men of ideas. This intellectual tenor toward frenzy is what drives them on. That's when *Death to the English!* is useless pomp and scrapped.

The lethargy at the end of combat leaves them thinking this.

Standing at the foot of the ramparts, she's surprised
to have been (for so long, considering her age) caught

not by her father, not by her mother,
not by the quest for food, nor the hypnotic chewing
of meals,
nor by food's final form,
not by the link with animals, when she's sleeping
among and eating with them, the ease of acting
like a cow without being one, bawling like a sheep,
scratching herself like a dog,
not by inhabiting:
the house, windows, door, the height of the threshold,
the length of the crack, the spaces between rivulets
running off roofs and the surface of puddles they
carve by stirring the dust;
the stupor of having *already* now *long ago* seen this,

but by a state of being, which includes all of this, in

which she herself is included, though she may look like she makes it up as she goes,

whereas here, today, everything that does not win the war (roads, negotiations, maps, meals, dressing, repairing, treating, sleeping) disappears in favor of a generalized *illico presto*: illico presto the assaults, illico presto the artillery, illico presto the fields, behind! right behind the horse! overwhelmed, illico presto at 6 o'clock in the morning, and at 7 o'clock, and 11 o'clock, and at 3 o'clock!

THE BLACK HORSEMAN – JOAN DARC

Zig-zag, arm up-arcing, circling, lunging my stallion, he spins around three times,
chimneys were blown down, and, as they say, lamentings heard i' the air, strange
do not follow my finger, three times I spin around, rough draft of
screams of death, and prophesying with accents terrible of dire combustion and
a duel, no part of my standard serves as a gourd, no backhand of gloves makes
confused events new hatch'd to the woful time: the obscure bird clamour'd the live
him jump, he's down! down! once on the ground, he cannot rise, because his armor
long night: some say, the earth was feverous and did shake. 'twas a rough night
is too heavy, although English-forged, he would need one aide, or two,
my young remembrance cannot parallel a fellow to it. O horror, horror, horror!
and everyone's too busy, just my luck, but, if I happen to fall
Tongue nor heart cannot conceive nor name thee. What's the matter? Confusion
myself, I'm in as hapless a quandary, neither time nor wit will aid me,
now hath made his masterpiece. Most sacrilegious murder hath broke ope the
what to do? impossible to speak while swinging my arm, it's surely useless to try to see

Lord's anointed temple, and stole thence the life o' the building. What is't you
let alone to distinguish, whoever this is, though his name be Black, he
say? The life? Mean you his majesty? Approach the chamber, and destroy your
is colorful enough, but covered in dust (due to the ardor), rough draft of a duel, surely,
sight with a new Gorgon: do not bid me speak; see, and then speak yourselves, ah!
ah! I will remember nothing from all this; in sum, what is it you want to have happened?
Ring the alarm-bell, murder and treason! Banco and Donalbain! Malcolm! awake!
Joan Darc! Joan Darc! Joan Darc! Jesus! on my honor and for my king! exhor
shake off this downy sleep, death's counterfeit, and look on death itself! up, up,
invoke, exhort, defy! when it's hardest, let your bones go to the Loire! not without
and see the great doom's image! As from your graves rise up, and walk like
the right, fluctuat: what's on my coat of arms! may your issue rot in your balls,
spirits! to countenance this horror. Ring the bell. What's the business, that such
to the thighs! to the knees! Spew yourself out piece by piece from your mouth,
a hideous trumpet calls to parley the sleepers of the house? Speak! speak!
Joan rain,   knights rain,   Joan rain!   knights rain!   Joan rain!

our traces: the runs, pellets, droppings, as scarce as a
badger's.

In the end, me heavy as a tree trunk toppled on
the ground, head wobbling

like the swollen bladder of a pig

Me, with feet twice the size of my hands.
Me, with my game shoulder.
Me the orator, 100 speeches in 100 days.
Me and my horse, and the blows I rain when he
falls.
Me, Joan, my chin nearing my brow (no teeth!)
PROUD – PURE – JOYOUS –
CONQUERING –
PROUD: is there a way to hunch over in armor?

PURE: water falling over my body has been blessed.

JOYOUS: the silent joy that greets me in the morning.

PROUD: jutting chin and feet in fighting stance.

PURE: after the war.

PROUD: everywhere always and I bring my horse.

PURE: I am clean in thought, word, and deed.

JOYOUS: smiling, mouth open, teeth golden from pollen caught in them.

Long before I mapped the route of my first campaign, I was already preparing the day before, at night in bed or in the morning as I woke, the route the flock would graze, the amount of wool to spin. I'd see eggs cracking open before dropping into the pan, and my thumbnail trying not to break a yolk.

– I've never sewn on a button without first seeing myself sewing on the button. This is how the needle finds the hole on the first poke; otherwise, right away and without thinking, it pricks something hard.

– It's not about strategy but *Self-possession*, and so I stay true and do not tremble.

– My voices are the prologue to my own *Self-possession*.

You see, there's real continuity in all of life's moments.

Within two lives of such differing intensities, treat all events the same: an assault like gathering a flock; calming the soldiers like scolding a dog (Joan adapts but she does not change).

– Her personality as shepherdess hasn't been loosed and lost along the way, but projected, expanded, and improved.

Thanks to the preceding days, we haven't lived in another country, or inhabited another house, not known a different father with a foreign name, not donned a dress we would never have worn, nor said hello in Breton.

– In any negotiation, there are a few key-words that should only be said standing up.

– The care I've taken to be seated correctly and to look my interlocutor straight in the eye changes my speech – "Make me a suit of armor," which I'd say standing up, becomes "I would like something with which to protect myself" when I'm sitting down.

– I quickly understood the advantage of speaking standing up.

– To explain my plan to my soldiers, I take a long stick, good for levelling the sand when drawing lines in it, and little square shapes for houses.

– Towns look flat from afar.
– You must give the brain time to recreate their depth.
– And don't forget that the plan for an attack (in two dimensions) will be three dimensional during the attack, and that you'll plunge into the drawing.

She went to war to end the war. She claimed that in seven years (her actual words were: "It won't take more than seven years for the war *to get winded*"), there'd be no more war.

– Truly, as long as the war hasn't ended, any claim that it will end in seven years seems more real than this war dragging on, which hovers between starting and stopping, cries and the cries of victory, hooray! no prisoners.

This claim cannot spare her from having to lie prone each morning in order to stretch out her sore back, aching from so much riding.

The extent of war in life without war is diminished, but persists in other forms. The warring life provides Joan with a homogenous look that nothing belies, where she feels neither too much nor nothing

for each morning her men wait at attention, horse halters looped over wrists.

(She mounts her horse.)

– To be on her horse galloping toward a town she'll prize open affirms her and the land – grass greener than green, houses, even the most decrepit huts, are houses, and she imagines their interiors, chairs and table in a single room with earthen floors, all while galloping by the vertical lines of slatted walls.

– Before the war, and before the *definition* it gives, houses are opaque, the people who live in them having closed off all access within, even to the imagination's plunder.

– Once you've spent years roaming, you never dream of rest (a wheel that stops rolling lies down on its side).

For the first part of her life, Joan was always careful to eat on just one side of her mouth (in essence the right).
She had only to think of using both sides of her mouth to get confused: trying to follow with her tongue then teeth the morsels' course, from right to left or the reverse, or in the middle the pulpy gruel, too soon to gulp and yet too late.

To spit or to swallow?
– to swallow, so she doesn't waste food,
or to spit, to combat mental tedium?
– to push it all over to the left, or to the right, if there's time?

And so the rule involved-evolved over her taste buds.

In war, however, where people make do and work fast, Joan often sees soldiers eating on both sides of their mouths.

Thanks to the process of analogy, Joan can explain
one thing by illustrating it with another:

Four eggs clapped on a plank are turrets, kidneys
serve as crenels, a watermelon equals the distance left
to cover (only two slices).

Handy, ordinary things, uncooked food providing
the small pawns, or elements, suitable for designing
encirclements, ruses, breaches.

– So her men see themselves in action, so she sees,
well ahead of time, what she must do.

She dips her arms in vinegar to make them fitter, firmer, and prettier, but also to leave the stories, mysterious, and to enter history, a more pointed fable in which young girls do not marry a king who builds an empire based on fleece.

In truth, she thinks about the sheer number of traits, names, physical characteristics of those significantly marginalized who came before, and makes her move.

She expects no unusual signs – sexual organs migrating to the side of the head, flies exorcised because they bite, turnips born in cauldrons –, and finds nothing so riveting as the growth of her own nails, but the amplitude's too faint to stir up anything but boredom: Charles' surprise at his coronation, his joy in an event assembling such colorful people, his wonder at hearing a secret I know about him, his frisson seeing me dressed in full armor, his fear at the idea of sudden mortal illness, his vision of the perfumed heart of Saint-Chrême in its shrine making him blush, before he is restored, cowed into place. *This is the bovine gait of the world.*

Here I am, credulous, high up on the pyre, reeking of
cresol,
myself reeking, running in my grease,
crepus-
cular before this crescendo that's killing me, before the
whole
herd of cretinous cretins

– Even though it was more useful to learn to write standing up, or on horseback (walk gait), being given (a chair) without further fuss, I sat on it, realizing at once I should write sitting down.

– My hand draws a big circle the index finger and thumb cannot close – the sword handle is not the nib of a quill.

– I often touch my lips.

– I hunch over less when I eat.

– I stop between each letter, never having thought of watching the skin on my fingers this close up.

– While I'm learning, as much as the letters I'm drawing, I observe the wood of the table, the paper as paper, the master, and with him: eyes, mouth (which moves), front teeth, collar, first button on the collar when I have just made a mistake.

– The time I wanted my eyes to follow the letter being formed, I could not finish it.

Jehanne

To go from the uncertain names of Tarc, Dare, Daire, of a girl who might have remained nameless – who would have been the shepherdess, the daughter of her father, a Domremian, a partisan, to the immunized Darc, Joan, you learned to acknowledge the D.A.R.C. as

Darc

Darc

Darc

Darc

Darc to duplicate, finally as sobriquet, the one you dreamed of: Angel Benefactor, Exterminator, Blonde Guardian, Gay and Patient Provider, Aide to Salvation, Soldier Lily, Loyal Standard, Unfailing Adjuvant, Linear and Wise Flower, Eye and Ear, Altar of Clairvoyance, Kind Enterprise, Prudent Victory, Image, Creatrix of Evidence, Gleaming Blade, Scourge of God.

– In Gien alone, half a dozen boys to baptize Charles, and girls to baptize Joan, wait on the church parvis for her to touch them with a finger dipped in holy water.

– Joan questions the wisdom of naming her future daughter Catherine, when everywhere the prestige and efficacy of the name Joan have been proved in battle, and, superimposed on the names Michael and Catherine, almost erased them.

– With the transformation she imposed on herself (horse, hair) through the conjugal influence of Michael and Catherine, she, Joan Darc, extracted herself, the girl, from an earlier and more infantile Joanie. Right now Joan the soldier watches and watches over the shepherdess.

– That's why Joan, daughter of Joan, can't name her future daughter Joan without robbing a part of her own past.

Hands down, I have never been patted so much since I was born as once I could read and negotiate, vive the rush! Cold or fevered, will you touch me when I'm flushed, helmet cool, hollows of my palms moist? I draw upon the auras of those who are hot as I in more than words, radiant, piercing me whether standing up or on all fours, visible across the whole northwest quarter of the country, able to leap from one side of a stream to the other, hop Lorraine hop Alsace, here is my treasure, the whole of me day and night, eddies and surges rising and falling unable to exit, my wrist, right, and my hand, open, ready for arms, my heart on a red cushion and a blue cloth, my tibia intact because I never broke a limb, these things you do not want to doubt.

Spreading the word that I'd shortened my hem was enough to set half the army to sewing.

Already, a young shepherd from Gévaudan: "Virgin, here I am, a young and able virgin, my hair shorn, my nape soft, my arms supple-jointed as ribbons, the English-French will fill the ditches on all the roads of France, so give me a horse that won't buck and armor that fits."

by dissimulation: "For four years (fourteen hundred 36), I've been a fake shepherd and fake virgin, but

my father Darc smacks me on the lips
when I return to the village,"

by assimilation:
Beatrice! called the Congolese Joan, and

Saint Catherine of Siena, Yves Nicolazie,
Suzette Labrousse and Catherine of La
Rochelle, Colette of Corbie, Pierrone of
Brittany and her companion, Marie of
Maillé, Robert Le Mennot, Marie Robine
called the Gasque of Avignon, Catherine
Sauve, the recluse of Lates harbor burned
at Montpellier, the vavasseur of Cham-
pagne, the Lady of Armoises, the maid of
Sarmaize, Jeanne la Féronne of Chassé-
les-Usson.

She thinks how lucky she is to have head facing forward (eyes, mouth, nose forward), because once when she was watching the sky without seeing a saint, she understood only later what she'd seen: two clouds moving slowly one toward the other on a blue with no surface no comfort.

A slight modification to her anatomy could make her a little less, or with more difficulty, Joan Darc:
– if her hands turned inside out, so she'd have to invent a new way to pray,
– if her eyes and mouth were pulled down to her belly, so she couldn't wear a helmet,
– if her legs were flexible as straps, so she couldn't mount a horse,
– if she had an immense upper lip, so she couldn't speak in negotiations,
– or if her mouth, ossified or too small, kept her from eating,
– if her arms were tied behind her ears, so she couldn't write or fight with ease.

Living with nose pressed to the glass, you see only later how you looked.

Sheep's wool, stony lanes, dog barks; but under this rustic surface, aren't there crowds of angels descending in cascades, swirling falls of thrones, saints gesturing from high up in trees, vortex, cantatas in patois?

My new life was superficially reversed, **baroque** on top: cavalcades, whirling blades, frenzied negotiations, strategies, trickery, drawings flecked with arrows, cries, armor… **austere** underneath: economy (wanting to be where you are the moment you are there), sole claim, interiorized ending, many prayers, and various muted things.

The visible break (first part of my life, second part of my life), was a kind of trope – once all the transitions, uncertainties, reversals receded – heightened to avert the fear, in the end, of being wishy-washy.

– Really, Joan, I understand that someone can commit herself to defending a cause, though it's lost, and though she reaps only censure and sarcasm, but to do it with such perseverance, such tenacity, it's a kind of perversion of the will, or a complicity so alien it's suspicious: you're too involved in all you do. You see, at some point, you have to accept who you are. You've gone to such lengths to escape your lot, now that you're about to accomplish what you said you would, it's time to face yourself. You have to know your own flaws, your virtues, your likes, your dislikes, and to leave no field fallow, as Gilles de Rais said.

Then, he returned to his castle.

Here
I am, credulous, high up on the pyre, reeking of cresol,
my-
self reeking, running my grease, crepuscular
be.
this crescendo that's killing me, before the whole
drove of

Around the time Margery Kempe arrives at Compostelle, Joan makes the same gesture to her jailers as the other made, this English woman who took to the road at forty after raising fourteen children, to her family: she cupped both breasts in her hands.

On the road, Margery observes towns and faces, noise, phenomena (climatic), interruptions, ways of taking a nap, recipes, baby babble, kitchen utensils, bridges, hats, cart tracks along the lanes, refrains, flora, insults, fauna, thinking of nothing besides writing her autobiography.

Darc travels, with all speed and no reserves, throwing away in the morning what she gathered the day before. Nothing is left but what she must do. She auto-cleans herself so her vigilance is flawless.

– It took time for me to realize that the clarity of war is found not in the assault, but in later recalling the events unfurling in chronological order.
– And that my predictions were actions.
– I saw them as surely as if I'd done them.
– And yet I had to do them.

It wasn't enough to see myself dressed as a man, they had to bring me male clothing, so I could dress as a man, and live right up to the end with the shame of having to explain why.

– And I had to justify my acts.
– In particular, the reason you cut your hair.
– It catches on the helmet.
– There's a will here to change the *person*, through a secondary sexual characteristic.
– With friction from the helmet, my hair was pulled out in fistfuls.
– The shaved nape!
– *Cutting my hair was faster than waiting for all my soldiers to grow theirs out.*

Actually, I take care of my horse and my horse takes care of me – though he can't move in my direction without butting me – and actually, I take care of the angels as they take care of me, they make me come here and I make them come here. They cannot be more here than what I have told you.

*

The more I observe what is here, whatever it is, the more force it has: the fennel I can see is more piercing than the cathedral I cannot see.

It hangs over me, it's so there I become the outside-of-fennel. Surely my situation isn't disgusting or even surprising, but sometimes, a vague foreboding makes me just want to get on with it.

In short, she was quite sure it was she who heard voices, and not her own voice heard by someone else somewhere across the vast world without her knowing it.

She never doubted it was her own voice that continued to issue between abdomen and throat, though so used to battle, to giving orders, it carried farther and farther, resonating in the open air as if in a church.

For a long time, she waited for the voices in fear – especially in the beginning, and oddly, at difficult times: she was always afraid of being yelled at.

– When she called them "voices," by the way, it was a manner of speaking. But try explaining what "voice" means when it does not mean voice.

– Can you imitate the voices that reach you?

– Does the voice come with an image, or can it sound alone, without any iconic aid?

– Is there one voice, speaking through the mouths of several saints, one saint with a multitude of voices, or does each saint have her own voice?

– Do they get angry?

– Do they change (intonation, timbre, cadence, spatial location) according to the nature of what they're saying?

– Did you ever have the impression that one was speaking to you without a voice?

– Do the saints always face you when they speak, or do they sometimes turn in profile?

– If not a virgin, would you be able to hear them?

– Have you ever been tempted to lose your virginity: never? rarely?

With all this riding I'm lucky I still have my maidenhead.

They did not give me the name of Maid by accident, the women can feel around all they want, inside me it holds, and twice over it holds.

– Indirectly, this name is the reason so many heads were lopped off.

And now look at them making their case between my legs.

– While they prove my virginity, I think back to the battles, the letters to the English, and how I should have written them.
– She thinks back to the days spent learning to read a map.
– And to the pea soup she vomited in the bushes before arriving at Gien.
– She thinks back to the ancient prayers:

King of Heaven, help me to enter a town without pitched battle, let the townsmen and

townswomen kneeling before their houses along the street await me, having slain and imprisoned manifold English, with their hands cut off.

And make Charles my king provide me with a strong army so I may see my mission through, and not this pack of rotten troops rejected by the Church, who curse and lag behind, not from fear but sloth. Make me no longer have to hire mercenaries, for I have no money.

And make them keep far away from me, and when they want to come near me, make their hands turn to ice and their fingers fall off like stalactites.

And make me be as hard as a wooden plate.

I am grateful to the court for the summons to appear before it because it wishes to reveal and to establish the truth, in order to know what has happened, and who has done what in this country.

– After hours and hours of arguments, intimidation, and threats of torture, in the end all that was left were the *toenails*.
– Before that, labyrinths of steps in dankness, and a dark darker than ordinary darkness
– along with the orders: right, and left, straight ahead, faster, faster.

Torturers are talkative.

I've learned what a corridor is because it's a new word, and the thing's very rare in the countryside.

Nothing goes on here, but, whether or not you've thought about it or despaired of it, it's an important place.

– The word *execution* was always spoken at the moment of execution, meaning, too late – *execution*, at the very moment one's falling.

A slow deterioration of the material situation, and the spiritual: in spite of the scale of the task accomplished, the accomplishment itself, and the idea that there's nothing more beyond this order, gives in retrospect the impression of a slow and certain deterioration.

SPIRITUAL: with her name, her virginity, her ideas, how can she be sitting here, counting, waiting for something to happen?

MATERIAL: the habit of smoothing her hair under her helmet has been replaced by rubbing her feet to remove sand from the prison floor.

SPIRITUAL: at prayer, her left hand rests loosely over her right.

MATERIAL: she loses weight, including from her arms.

SPIRITUAL: she can't remember her dog's name. What would she do if he didn't come when she called?

MATERIAL: she coughs. Coughing, she breathes and speaks less.

SPIRITUAL: *I defended these swine,*
Rouen, round of swine,
Tripe, scrap, scum.

MATERIAL: the calluses on her fingers from arms and quill have shrunk, but now a terrible rheumatism roams her hands.

SPIRITUAL: during the day thoughts come which seem strange only in retrospect: is there any objective reason why I am not a *rabbit?*

MATERIAL: in the eyes and the ears, there's no poverty that doesn't show up early on in the ears and the eyes: oozing, clogging, semi-deafness, veiling, blurring, spots. Perfect hearing and sight invite us to war – blind men are never generals; the canteen cook must answer the soldier without raising her eyes from the soup.

SPIRITUAL: she hears *Joan, you answer, but you do not hear what is said to you. You're really so convinced that you hear the voices of God that you do not hear those of men. And those of God, which you claim to transmit* MATERIAL *are replaced by your own, which proclaims you, and administers to you, always first: The Maid speaks in the name of the Maid, and promises many battles, and many heads cut off. The Maid* SPIRITUAL *delivers blame and praise, and baptizes the girls "Joan." The Maid "crowns" a king. The people believe in you, war leader. Should they believe in the leader, or in God? – You say the one, but you do the other.*

*And you say that a personal miracle, a vocation, can guide a life from beginning to end*MATERIAL*Even the uncertainty of the war and its sides has taught you nothing. You appear before your judges just as you could have appeared leaving Domrémy. Exhausted, you speak without thinking about what is happening to you. What's more, you think nothing will happen to you other than what you've predicted. You are alone; a whole army couldn't take this solitude away from you*

And when her thoughts turn to the past, she sees herself there, a shepherdess, already exhausted.

Perpetual crowding and perpetual isolation, there are few things and few people who aren't too close or too far away.

Rancid in Paris, rancid in Domrémy,

rancid Blandine, rancid Abelard and Eloise
rancid Roland, and rancid Roncevaux
the rancid Saracens
rancid Judas and Jesus
Charles the rancid
rancid Pisan Christine de
rancid Cicero, Caesar.

– Here's Joan drawing herself up forever tall against the sky with a stake at her back.

– Each vertebra presses against the trunk as if to enter it.

– The wind does not ruffle her dress, because of the ropes.

Of the kind of tree that shores her (oak? beech? alder? willow?), we know nothing, because it burned with her.

– Her final expression, hard to read on a face in flames: either dolorous, or joyous, or dolorous and joyous.

Can we see blood running down the burning body?

– A contemporary questions whether someone could pleasure and suffer at the same time, whether jouissance and sufferance alternate, one rising as the other recedes.

The crowd forms a cresting sea before her. She can clearly see a little towhead.

In the center of the confusion, she is both calm and deaf (no cry filters through those wide open mouths).

– A course patiently pursued – from Domrémy to Auxerre, Gien to Bourges, Sens to Paris, Reims to Soissons, Arras to Rouen – starts its final progress, from feet to ankles, knees to soft thighs, nipple to neck's nape, vibrant chin to trembling nostrils (then from her mouth soars the dove).

– Lunula or patella, nothing's discreet anymore, this is a young (vain?) and compact body burning up, joyous blaze, mystic barbecue.

– Her spasmodic breathing is stopped by the coughing.
– And her eyes turn in their orbits.

.

Acknowledgments

Our deep thanks to the editors of the following journals for publishing excerpts from *Joan Darc*, sometimes in earlier versions:

The untitled poems beginning "Dressed in armor, Joan" "Before my first assault," "our traces: the runs," "Here I am, credulous," "Even though it was more useful," and the poem entitled "The Black Horseman – Joan Darc," were published in *asymptote* (January 2015). Electronic journal.

The untitled poems beginning "Joan," "your knees will guide horses," "Why when she's standing around," "She dreams up new forms of assault," and "To go from the uncertain names," were published in *Waxwing 2* (Spring 2014). Electronic journal.

Poetry International (Fall 2016) excerpted *Joan Darc* in a special portfolio section that was composed of the reprinted untitled poems beginning "Joan," "your knees will guide horses," and "Before my first assault," as well as the following untitled poems beginning "With a panorama at the center," "Joan only loves herself," "Like most of the villagers," "Viewed from the outside," "The sword's hilt,"

"She went to war," "Living with nose pressed," "Really, Joan,"
"It took time for me," "In sum, she," "Can you imitate," "After
hours and hours," "A slow deterioriation," and "Here's Joan
drawing." Print.

We are profoundly grateful to the National Endowment
for the Arts, which awarded us a Fellowship in Translation
in 2015 to complete this translation, and to Cole Swensen,
poet, translator, and publisher extraordinaire of La Presse,
for the invitation to undertake this project and the expertise
she shared as we completed it. That has made all the dif-
ference! For making herself available for consultations as
we worked on the translation, we thank the Nathalie
Quintane scholar, Jodie M. Barker, whose knowledge of
Quintane's oeuvre was invaluable; as well as Quintane her-
self, whose remarkable poem never ceased to fascinate and
challenge us, and who so generously answered our many
questions. Deep thanks to The Anderson Center, where
this translation was completed during a one-month resi-
dency in 2016, and to its Executive Director, the distin-
guished poet and translator Christopher Burawa, who gave
the penultimate version a crucial, thorough final edit with
generous feedback and notes. Finally, I have a chance to
thank my colleague and team-teacher in literary translation
at Arizona State University, Paul Morris, who first came
to me with the idea of developing a translation seminar a
decade ago – and what a decade it has been! Lastly, deep
gratitude to the Maxine and Jonathan Marshall Chair in
Poetry and the Department of English, which provided

funding to travel to France over three summers, during which time we began and then advanced our work on *Joan Darc*.

This is the sixteenth title in the La Presse series
of contemporary French poetry in translation.
The series is edited by Cole Swensen. The
book is set in Adobe Jenson, and
is designed by Shari DeGraw.